Canine Cuisine Cookbook

Simple, Wholesome Homemade Dog Food Recipes

Table of Contents

Introduction

When you make your dog's food at home, you can control the ingredients that go into it. You can also be sure that the meat you are using is of good quality. Making your own dog food is not as hard as it may seem, and it is a great way to ensure that your dog is getting the healthy food they deserve.

If you're looking for a way to show your dog some extra love, then this is the cookbook for you! All of the recipes inside are made with whole, natural ingredients and are designed to be easy and quick to make, usually in less than designed to be easy and quick to make, usually in less than 15 minutes. Plus, your dog will love the new flavors and variety.

Each recipe in "*Canine Cuisine Cookbook*" has had its components double-checked to ensure they are safe for canines, and several canine taste testers have given their stamp of approval. So, what will be the first dish you prepare for your dog? A simple chicken dinner? A refreshing summer smoothie, perhaps? Or you could kick things off with a dog burger; either way, you're guaranteed success. To your dog: Call me over and tell me they'll soon be enjoying homemade, tasty food every day!

Recipe 1. Pup Chili

Yield: 10 cups

Active Time: 15 minutes

Ingredient List:

1. 1/3 cup tomato paste
2. 1 can drained and rinsed black beans
3. 1 pound ground lean beef

4. 1 cup chopped carrots

5. 1 pound ground turkey

6. 2 cups of chicken broth

7. 1 can drained and rinsed red kidney beans

8. 2 cups of water

9. 1/2 cup corn kernels

Instructions:

Step 1   Place the ground beef and ground turkey in a nonstick skillet and sear for about 5 minutes, breaking it apart with a spatula as it cooks.

Step 2   Move the chicken to a large pot and add all the remaining ingredients.

Step 3   Bring the mix to a boil and simmer for 10 minutes.

Step 4   Remove from the heat and allow the chili to cool. Serve to your pup right away or store in the fridge or freezer to use later!

Recipe 2. Fall Specialty

Yield: About 16 cups

Active Time: 5 minutes

Ingredient List:

1. 6 cups of ground turkey (three pounds)
2. 2 cups of frozen Brussel sprouts
3. 1 cup of frozen corn kernels

4. 1 cup of frozen chopped pumpkin

5. 2 cups of brown rice

6. 4 cups of chicken broth

7. 2 cups of canned red kidney beans, liquid drained, beans rinsed

Instructions:

Step 1   Place all of the ingredients into a slow cooker and stir slightly.

Step 2   Cook on high for 4 hours, stirring occasionally if you are able. You can also opt to set the slow cooker to low heat and cook for 6 hours.

Step 3   Let the food cool and serve or freeze for later!

Recipe 3. Turkey Burgers

Yield: 6 Burgers

Active Time: 10 minutes

Ingredient List:

1. 1/4 cup of grated parmesan cheese

2. 1/4 cup of low fat cottage cheese

3. 1 pound of ground turkey (opt for a leaner turkey if possible)

4. 1/2 cup of carrots

5. 1 cup of peas

6. 2 eggs

7. 1 cup of oats

Instructions:

Step 1   Mix all the ingredients together in a bowl. Use your hands to really ensure that everything is well mixed.

Step 2   Form the burgers into patties and bake in a 350-degree oven for 10 minutes, flipping them over and bake for another 5 minutes. Baking the burgers to make sure you use less oil; however, grilling the burgers is also a great option.

Step 3   Let the burger cool and give it to your pup! These also freeze well for use later.

Recipe 4. Creamy Fruit and Vegetable

Yield: 7 cups of food

Active Time: 10 minutes

Ingredient List:

1. 1 cup of peas

2. 1/2 cup of water

3. 1 cup of chopped green beans

4. 1 cup of chopped carrots

5. 3 cups of cooked brown rice

6. 2 bananas

7. 3 cups of millet, already cooked per package
    directions

Instructions:

Step 1   In a large pot or Dutch oven, adding the cooked
          rice and cooked millet along with the water. Stir
          to combine and heat over medium heat until
          simmering and let cook for 5 minutes.

Step 2   In a blender, mixing the
          remaining ingredients and blend until smooth.
          Add the pureed veggies to the grain mix and stir.

Step 3   Serve to your pup while warm but not hot. Store
          in the fridge or freeze until ready to serve!

Recipe 5. Veggie Treats

Yield: 40 Treats

Active Time: 15 minutes

Ingredient List:

1. 1 cooked and peeled sweet potato
2. 1/2 cup of peas
3. 1/4 cup of warm water
4. 2 cups of flour (preferably whole wheat)

5. 1 cup of chopped and cooked carrots

6. 1/2 cup of applesauce

7. 1/2 cup of green beans

8. 3/4 cup of oats

Instructions:

Step 1   Place the carrots and sweet potato in a food processor and puree until smooth.

Step 2   Add the remaining ingredients into the food processor and pulse until a dough begins to form.

Step 3   Roll the dough on a lightly floured surface to about 1/8 of an inch thick. Then, using a knife or pizza cutter to cut the dough into long strips.

Step 4   Place the strips on a lined cookie sheet and bake in a 350 degrees Fahrenheit oven for 25 minutes.

Step 5   Break the strips into small pieces for your dog and serve once cooled.

Recipe 6. Beef Veggie

Yield: 8 cups of food

Active Time: 30 minutes

Ingredient List:

1. 1 1/2 pounds of lean ground beef
2. 3/4 cup of diced or shredded carrots (frozen of fresh)
3. 2 cups of spinach

4. 1 cup of brown rice

5. 1 cup of grated zucchini

6. 1 tablespoon of olive oil

7. 1/2 cup of frozen peas

Instructions:

Step 1   Begin by cooking the brown rice according to the package directions. Once it is cooked, setting the rice aside to cook and proceed with the recipe.

Step 2   Using a large pot, heating the oil until it begins to simmer. Once hot, adding the ground beef to the pot and break up the pieces using a rubber spatula or wooden spoon.

Step 3   Cook the lean ground beef, stirring frequently for about 5 minutes or until there is not pink left, and the turkey is nicely browned.

Step 4   Add the remaining ingredients and stir until cooked. The spinach should be wilted and the carrots and zucchini soft.

Step 5   Turn the heat off from the stove and add the cooked rice to the turkey mixture. Stir everything together and allow to cool.

Recipe 7. Berry Smoothie

Yield: 8 cups

Active Time: 5 minutes

Ingredient List:

1. 2 cups of cooked brown rice

2. 2 whole bananas

3. 1 cup of chopped strawberries

4. 1 cup of water

5.   1 cup of blueberries

6.   1 cup of raspberries

Instructions:

Step 1   Place all ingredients into a blender and puree until smooth. Add a little extra water if needed to make the mix thinner. If you would like the mix to be a little thicker for your pup, adding a little browner rice.

Step 2   Serve to your dog cold, almost frozen to help them cool down in the summer heat.

Step 3   Store in the fridge or freezer until ready to eat!

Recipe 8. Turkey Veggie

Yield: 8 cups of food

Active Time: 30 minutes

Ingredient List:

1. 1 cup of grated zucchini

2. 3/4 cup of diced or shredded carrots (frozen of fresh)

3. 1 1/2 pound of ground Turkey

4. 1 cup of brown rice

5. 1 tablespoon of olive oil

6. 2 cups of spinach

Instructions:

Step 1	Begin by cooking the brown rice according to the package directions. Once it is cooked, setting the rice aside to cook and proceed with the recipe.

Step 2	Using a large pot, heating the oil until it begins to simmer. Once it is hot, adding the turkey to the pot and break up the pieces using a rubber spatula or wooden spoon.

Step 3	Cook the turkey, stirring frequently for about 5 minutes or until there is not pink left and the turkey is nicely browned.

Step 4	Add the remaining ingredients and stir until cooked. The spinach should be wilted and the carrots and zucchini soft.

Step 5	Turn the heat off from the stove and add the cooked rice to the turkey mixture. Stir everything together and allow to cool.

Recipe 9. Chicken Chili

Yield: 8 cups

Active Time: 15 minutes

Ingredient List:

1. 2 cups of chicken broth
2. 1 can of black beans, drained and rinsed
3. 3 pounds of chicken breast
4. 2 cups of water

5. 1 can of drained and rinsed red kidney beans,

6. 1/3 cup of tomato paste

Instructions:

Step 1   Trim any fat off from the chicken breast and then cut it into small, one-inch pieces. Place the chicken in a sauté pan and sear for about 2 minutes on each side, just until the outside is no longer pink.

Step 2   Move the chicken to a large pot and add all the remaining ingredients.

Step 3   Bring the mix to boil then simmer for 10 minutes.

Step 4   Remove from the heat and allow the chili to cool. Serve to your pup right away or store in the fridge or freezer to use later!

Recipe 10. Turkey Jerky

Yield: about 16 strips

Active Time: 5 minutes

Ingredient List:

1.   4 Turkey Breasts

Instructions:

Step 1   Slice the turkey breast into thing, 1/16-inch strips and place on a baking sheet lined with a silicone mat.

Step 2   Bake the strips in a 200 degrees Fahrenheit oven for 2 hours, flipping after 1 1/2 hour and cooking the remaining 30 minutes.

Step 3   Cool the jerky and store in an airtight container in the refrigerator for up to 2 weeks.

Recipe 11. Slow Cooker Chicken

Yield: About 16 cups

Active Time: 5 minutes

Ingredient List:

1.   2 cups of canned red kidney beans, liquid drained, beans rinsed

2.   1 cup of frozen chopped carrots

3.   2 cups of brown rice

4. 1 cup of green beans

5. 1 cup of frozen chopped sweet potato

6. 6 cups of ground chicken (3 pounds)

7. 1 cup of frozen peas

8. 4 cups of chicken broth

Instructions:

Step 1   Place all of the ingredients into a slow cooker and stir slightly.

Step 2   Cook on high heat for 4 hours, stirring occasionally if you are able. You can also opt to set the slow cooker to low heat and cook for 6 hours.

Step 3   Let the food cool and serve or freeze for later!

Recipe 12. Chicken Veggie Treats

Yield: 20 treats

Active Time: 15 minutes

Ingredient List:

1. 1/2 cup of whole wheat flour

2. 1/2 cup of cooked peas

3. 1 cup water

4. 1 1/2 cups of pureed cooked chicken

5. 2 cups of dry milk powder

6. 1/2 cup cooked corn kernels

7. 1/2 cup of rolled oats

Instructions:

Step 1   Mix all of the ingredients together in a large bowl, stirring until everything is fully combined.

Step 2   Scoop the mix onto a parchment lined cookie sheet and ice cream scoop to ensure each treat is the same size.

Step 3   Bake in a 350 degrees Fahrenheit oven for 15 minutes.

Step 4   Allow the treats to fully cool before tossing one to your pup.

Step 5   Store the treats in the fridge, wrapped for up to 5 days.

Recipe 13. Beef Stew

Yield: 6 cups of stew

Active Time: 10 minutes

Ingredient List:

1. 1/2 cup of chopped green beans
2. 4 cups of water
3. 1 pound of ground beef
4. 1 cup of diced sweet potato

5. 2 cups of beef broth

6. 1/2 cup of chopped carrots

Instructions:

Step 1 Add all of the ingredients to a large saucepot and bring to a simmer over medium heat.

Step 2 Simmer the stew for 30 minutes, stirring occasionally, until the potatoes are soft, and the meat is no longer pink.

Step 3 Cool the stew until it is room temperature and give a nice big bowl to your pups!

Recipe 14. Frozen Peanut Butter Cubes

Yield: 36 cubes

Active Time: 5 minutes

Ingredient List:

1. 1 cup of peanut butter
2. 1/4 cup of whole milk plain yogurt
3. 1/4 cup of water

Instructions:

Step 1   Blend all the ingredients together in a food
          processor or blender until it smooth.

Step 2   Pour into an ice cube tray or small silicone mold
          and freeze for 4 hrs. or until it becomes frozen
          solid.

Step 3   Pop out a cube anytime you need a treat for your
          dog!

Recipe 15. Dog Crunchies

Yield: 20 Snacks

Active Time: 10 minutes

Ingredient List:

1.   20 thinly sliced strawberries
2.   5 thinly sliced bananas

Instructions:

Step 1   Thinly slice the strawberries and bananas and lay them on the trays of a dehydrator. Each piece of fruit should be separate and not overlapping or touching.

Step 2   Dehydrate the fruit according to your manufacturer's directions. Store the treats in an airtight container and toss a few to your dog anytime they deserve a treat!

Recipe 16. Slow Cooker Veggie

Yield: About 16 cups

Active Time: 5 minutes

Ingredient List:

1. 2 cups of brown rice

2. 1 cup of diced sweet potato

3. 1 cup of green beans

4. 2 cups of canned red kidney beans, liquid drained, beans rinsed

5. 2 cups of frozen chopped carrots

6. 1 cup of frozen chopped sweet potato

7. 4 cups of water

8. 1 cup of frozen peas

9. 1 cup of diced Idaho potato

Instructions:

Step 1   Place all of the ingredients into a slow cooker and stir slightly.

Step 2   Cook on high heat for 4 hours, stirring occasionally if you are able. You can also opt to set the slow cooker to low heat and cook for 6 hours.

Step 3   Let the food cool and serve or freeze for later!

Recipe 17. Vegan Dog Food

Yield: 7 Cups

Active Time: 10 minutes

Ingredient List:

1. 1 cup of peas

2. 1/2 cup of water

3. 3 cups of millet, already cooked per package directions

4. 1 cup of chopped green beans

5. 1 cup of chopped carrots

6. 3 cups of cooked brown rice

Instructions:

Step 1   In a large pot or Dutch oven, add the cooked rice and cooked millet along with the water. Stir to combine. Heat over medium heat until simmering and let cook for 5 minutes.

Step 2   In a blender, mix the remaining ingredients and blend until smooth. Add the pureed veggies to the grain mix and stir.

Step 3   Serve to your pup while warm but not hot. Store in the fridge or freeze until ready to serve!

Recipe 18. The Chicken Basics

Yield: 8 cups of food

Active Time: 5 minutes

Ingredient List:

1. 1 1/2 pounds of lean ground chicken
2. 2 1/2 cups of brown rice
3. 1/2 cup of frozen carrots
4. 1/2 cup of frozen peas

5. 5 1/2 cups of chicken broth (or water if your dog is
    sensitive to chicken)

Instructions:

Step 1   Place all the ingredients in a large pot and stir
          briefly.

Step 2   Bring the mix to a boil over the high heat and
          lower the heat to medium low and let the mix
          simmer for about 25 minutes.

Step 3   Remove the pot from the heat and stir. The rice
          should be fully cooked, and all the broth or water
          should be dissolved.

Step 4   Allow the food to cool and then refrigerate or
          cool until your dog is ready to eat!

Recipe 19. Salmon Veggie

Yield: 8 cups of food

Active Time: 30 minutes

Ingredient List:

1. 1 cup of frozen corn kernels
2. 2 cups of spinach
3. 1 cup of grated zucchini
4. 1/2 cup of frozen peas

5. 1 tablespoon of olive oil

6. 1 cup of brown rice

7. 3/4 cup of diced or shredded carrots (frozen of fresh)

8. 1 1/2 pounds of salmon

Instructions:

Step 1   Begin by cooking the brown rice according to the package directions. Once it is cooked, setting the rice aside to cook and proceed with the recipe.

Step 2   Using a large pot, heating the oil until it begins to simmer. Once it is hot, adding the salmon to the pot and cook for about 5 minutes on one side, flipping the filets, and cooking for another 3 minutes on the other side.

Step 3   Once the salmon is cooked, break it apart into flaky pieces using a fork or spatula.

Step 4   Add the remaining ingredients and stir until cooked. The spinach should be wilted and the corn, peas, and carrots soft.

Step 5   Turn the heat off from the stove and add the cooked rice to the turkey mixture. Stir everything together and allow to cool.

Recipe 20. Orange Indulgence

Yield: About 16 cups

Active Time: 5 minutes

Ingredient List:

1.   4 cups of water

2.   2 cups of brown rice

3.   1 cup of frozen chopped pumpkin

4.   1 cup of peeled and chopped sweet potato

5. 6 cups of ground chicken (three pounds)

6. 2 cups of frozen carrots

7. 2 cups of canned garbanzo beans, liquid drained, beans rinsed

Instructions:

Step 1   Place all of the ingredients into a slow cooker and stir slightly.

Step 2   Cook on high for 4 hours, stirring occasionally if you are able. You can also opt to set the slow cooker to low heat and cook for 6 hours.

Step 3   Let the food cool and serve or freeze for later!

Recipe 21. The Turkey Basics

Yield: 8 cups of food

Active Time: 5 minutes

Ingredient List:

1.   1/2 cup of frozen peas

2.   1 1/2 pounds of lean ground turkey

3.   5 1/2 cups of chicken broth (or water if your dog is sensitive to chicken)

4. 1/2 cup of frozen carrots

5. 2 1/2 cups of brown rice

Instructions:

Step 1   Place all the ingredients into a large pot and stir briefly.

Step 2   Bring the mix to a boil over the high heat and then lower the heat to medium low and let the mix simmer for about 25 minutes.

Step 3   Remove the pot from the heat and stir. The rice should be fully cooked, and all the broth or water should be dissolved.

Step 4   Allow the food to cool and then refrigerate or cool until your dog is ready to eat!

Recipe 22. Meaty Mix

Yield: 8 cups of food

Active Time: 30 minutes

Ingredient List:

1. 1 cup of grated zucchini
2. 1 cup of brown rice
3. 1/2 pound of lean ground chicken
4. 1 tablespoon of olive oil

5. 1/2 pound of lean ground beef

6. 1/2 pound of ground Turkey

7. 2 cups of spinach

8. 3/4 cup of diced or shredded carrots (frozen of fresh)

Instructions:

Step 1   Begin by cooking the brown rice according to the package directions. Once it is cooked, setting the rice aside to cook and proceed with the recipe.

Step 2   Using a large pot, heat the oil until it begins to simmer. Once it is hot, add the turkey, beef, and chicken to the pot and break up the pieces using a rubber spatula or wooden spoon.

Step 3   Cook the meats, stirring frequently for about 5 minutes or until there is not pink left and the turkey is nicely browned.

Step 4   Add the remaining ingredients and stir until cooked. The spinach should be wilted and the carrots and zucchini soft.

Step 5   Turn the heat off from the stove and add the cooked rice to the turkey mixture. Stir everything together and allow to cool.

Recipe 23. Doggy Burgers

Yield: 6 Burgers

Active Time: 10 minutes

Ingredient List:

1. 1/2 cup of carrots

2. 1 pound of ground beef (opt for a leaner beef if possible)

3. 1/4 cup of low-fat cottage cheese

4. 1 cup of oats

5. 1/4 cup of grated parmesan cheese

6. 1 cup of peas

7. 2 eggs

Instructions:

Step 1   Mix all the ingredients together in a bowl. Use your hands to really ensure that everything is well mixed.

Step 2   Form the burgers into patties and bake in a 350 degrees oven for 10 minutes, flipping them and then bake for another 5 minutes. Baking the burgers makes sure you use less oil; however, grilling the burgers is also a great option.

Step 3   Let the burger cool and give it to your pup! These also freeze well for use later

Recipe 24. Chicken Stew

Yield: 6 cups of stew

Active Time: 10 minutes

Ingredient List:

1.	1/2 cup of chopped carrots

2.	2 cups of beef broth

3.	1 pound of ground chicken

4.	1/2 cup of diced Idaho potatoes

5. 4 cups of water

6. 1/2 cup of chopped green beans

7. 1 cup of diced sweet potato

Instructions:

Step 1   Add all of the ingredients to a large saucepot and bring to simmer over medium heat.

Step 2   Simmer the stew for 30 minutes, stirring occasionally, until the potatoes are soft, and the meat is no longer pink.

Step 3   Cool the stew until it is room temperature and give a nice big bowl to your pup!

Recipe 25. Dog Pops

Yield: 8 cups

Active Time: 5 minutes

Ingredient List:

1. 1 cup of chopped strawberries
2. 2 cups of whole plain milk yogurt
3. 1 cup of blueberries
4. 1 peeled and chopped whole bananas

Instructions:

Step 1   Place all ingredients into a blender and puree until smooth.

Step 2   pour the mix into popsicle molds and freeze for about 5 hours or until hard.

Step 3   Serve to your dog cold to help them cool down in the summer heat. Be sure to keep an eye on your dog as they lick the pop, don't let them swallow the whole thing!

Step 4   Store in the freezer until ready to eat!

Recipe 26. Beef and Veggie Treats

Yield: 20 treats

Active Time: 15 minutes

Ingredient List:

1. 1 1/2 cups of cooked pureed beef
2. 1/2 cup of rolled oats
3. 1/2 cup of cooked peas
4. 1 cup of water

5. 1/2 cup of whole wheat flour

6. 2 cups of dry milk powder

Method:

Step 1   Mix all of the ingredients together in a large bowl, stirring until everything is fully combined.

Step 2   Scoop the mix onto a parchment lined cookie sheet and ice cream scoop to ensure each treat is the same size.

Step 3   Bake in a 350 degrees Fahrenheit oven for 15 minutes.

Step 4   Allow the treats to fully cool before tossing one to your pup.

Step 5   Store the treats in the fridge, wrapped for up to 5 days.

Recipe 27. Fruit and Veggie Strips

Yield: 40 Treats

Active Time: 15 minutes

Ingredient List:

1. 1/4 cup of warm water

2. 3/4 cup of oats

3. 1 cup of chopped and cooked carrots

4. 1/2 cup of applesauce

5. 1 large banana

6. 2 cups of flour (preferably whole wheat)

7. 1 cooked and peeled sweet potato

Instructions:

Step 1   Place the banana and sweet potato in a food processor and puree until smooth.

Step 2   Add the remaining ingredients into the food processor and pulse until a dough begins to form.

Step 3   Roll the dough on a lightly floured surface to about 1/8 of an inch thick. Then, using a knife or pizza cutter to cut the dough into long strips.

Step 4   Place the strips on a lined cookie sheet and bake in a 350 degrees Fahrenheit oven for 25 minutes.

Step 5   Break the strips into small pieces for your dog and serve once cooled.

Recipe 28. Pumpkin Treats

Yield: 36 cubes

Active Time: 5 minutes

Ingredient List:

1. 1/4 cup of water

2. 1 cup of chopped cooked pumpkin

3. 1/8 teaspoon of cinnamon

4. 1/4 cup of whole milk plain yogurt

Instructions:

Step 1   Blend all the ingredients together in a blender or
          food processor until smooth.

Step 2   Freeze for 4 hours or until frozen firm in an ice
          cube tray or tiny silicone mold.

Step 3   Pop out a cube anytime you need a treat for your
          dog!

Recipe 29. Creamy Chicken and Vegetable

Yield: 7 cups of food

Active Time: 10 minutes

Ingredient List:

1.   1 cup of cooked ground chicken

2.   1/2 cup of water

3.   1 cup of chopped green beans

4. 1 cup of peas

5. 3 cups of millet, already cooked per package directions

6. 1 cup of chopped carrots

7. 3 cups of cooked brown rice

Instructions:

Step 1   In a large pot or Dutch oven, adding the cooked rice and cooked millet along with the water. Stir to combine and heat over medium heat until simmering and let it cook for 5 minutes.

Step 2   In a blender, mixing the remaining ingredients and blend until smooth. Add the pureed veggies to the grain mix and stir.

Step 3   Serve to your pup while warm but not hot. Store in the fridge or freeze until ready to serve!

Recipe 30. Summer Smoothie

Yield: 8 cups

Active Time: 5 minutes

Ingredient List:

1. 1 cup of water
2. 1 cup of blueberries
3. 1 cup of cantaloupe
4. 2 whole bananas

5. 2 cups of cooked brown rice

6. 1 cup of chopped strawberries

Instructions:

Step 1   Place all ingredients into a blender and puree until smooth. Add a little extra water if needed to make the mix thinner. If you would like the mix to be a little thicker for your pup, adding a little browner rice.

Step 2   Serve to your dog cold, almost frozen to help them cool down in the summer heat.

Step 3   Store in the fridge or freezer until ready to eat!